Original title:
Inlaid Candles Among the Witch Cage

Author: Johan Kirsipuu
ISBN HARDBACK: 978-1-80559-473-4
ISBN PAPERBACK: 978-1-80559-972-2

Visions in the Shade of Flickering Light

In the corner, shadows dance,
Whispers weave a secret chance.
Flickering light casts dreams anew,
Painting visions, bright and few.

Through the veil of twilight's grace,
Echoes linger, time's embrace.
Each soft glow reveals a path,
Guiding souls from shadow's wrath.

Leaves rustle in the evening air,
Carried whispers of silent prayer.
Hearts untangle, softly sigh,
In the shade where shadows lie.

A Tapestry of Glow in Magical Silence

Stars weave stories in the night,
A tapestry of glow, pure delight.
In the hush, the world seems bright,
Magic lingers, hearts take flight.

Moonbeams stitch the night's embrace,
Crafting dreams in timeless space.
Every twinkle sings a tune,
Filling hearts with sweet monsoon.

Silent whispers, the wind does carry,
In still moments, the soul can tarry.
A gentle touch, a soft caress,
In this glow, we find our rest.

Secrets of the Hidden Firekeeper

Deep within the forest glade,
Lives a keeper, unafraid.
With each flicker, secrets flare,
Guarding flames with utmost care.

Stories whispered in the night,
Of the fire, fierce and bright.
Embers glow with ancient lore,
Scattering tales forevermore.

In the shadows, wisdom sleeps,
While the guardian vigil keeps.
Mysteries wrapped in crackling heat,
An eternal cycle, bold and sweet.

Between Shadow and Flicker: A Quiet War

In the twilight, shadows crawl,
Silent battles, whispers call.
Flickers clash in quiet grace,
A dance of light, a solemn race.

Veils of dusk conceal the strife,
Where shadows yearn for hidden life.
In this game, the light must bend,
As flickering hopes begin to blend.

Against the dark, the flames will rise,
Casting dreams before our eyes.
In the quiet, victory speaks,
As the heart, with courage, seeks.

Spellbound Brightness in the Heart of Night

In the depths where shadows play,
Stars whisper secrets of the day.
Moonlight dances on the ground,
While dreams weave softly all around.

A silver glow ignites the gloom,
Chasing away the silent doom.
Hearts awaken to the sight,
Spellbound brightness in the night.

Whispers carried on the breeze,
Melodies that bring us ease.
Each twinkle holds a story bright,
A journey into pure delight.

Night-lights sprinkle hope anew,
Painting skies with shades of blue.
In this realm where magic's free,
We find our truest harmony.

So let the darkness close its gates,
For in our souls, the light awaits.
Under stars, we feel the spark,
Spellbound brightness in the dark.

Captive Flickers in the Witch's Domain

In the shadows where the witches weave,
Flickers spark, tempting to believe.
Candlelight in corners creep,
Secrets that the night will keep.

Potions simmer, whispers blend,
Flickering flames, the air they mend.
Through the haze, the spirits flow,
Captive flickers dance and glow.

Echoes of a long-lost lore,
In every flicker, tales galore.
Through ancient woods where shadows tread,
The witch's magic, softly spread.

A cauldron bubbles with intent,
Here, every flicker's a lament.
In her lair, the world stands still,
Captive candles, bending will.

Beware the charm that ensnares the mind,
For in her grasp, the truth you'll find.
In her domain, the flickers gleam,
Bound by magic, held in dream.

Mysteries of Light Within Bound Rituals

In the silence where the candles burn,
Mysteries of light take their turn.
Chants echo softly in the night,
Binding shadows with purest light.

Ancient runes upon the floor,
Each drawn line opens a door.
With every breath, the tension grows,
Light within rituals gently flows.

Veils of secrecy shroud the space,
As spirits gather, the light will trace.
In circles drawn, intentions rise,
Mysteries unfold before our eyes.

Within this haven, fear subsides,
As the glowing essence guides.
From every heart, a silent wish,
Fulfilling the forbidden bliss.

Through the darkness, the flames invite,
To know the power of hidden might.
In bound rituals, we unite,
Mysteries of light, pure and bright.

Luminous Enchantment Behind Enchanted Grills

Behind the bars of twisted iron,
Lies a world where dreams are sired.
Luminous shadows weave and swirl,
Guarding secrets of a hidden pearl.

Softly glowing hearts align,
With each pulse, the worlds entwine.
Through the gaps, the echoes hum,
Enchantment whispers, calling some.

Captured light dances in delight,
Behind enchanted grills, the night.
A tapestry of colors blend,
Where beginnings and endings bend.

Each flicker tells a fleeting tale,
Of adventures that cannot fail.
In this realm, we find our place,
Luminous magic, sweet embrace.

So stand enchanted by the glow,
Let your heart with wonders flow.
Behind these bars, the life unfurls,
Luminous enchantment, endless pearls.

Keeper of Shadows with Illuminated Love

In the night where whispers dance,
The keeper guards with hollow glance.
Light entwines in shadows deep,
A love that whispers, secrets keep.

Stars above in quiet song,
Guide the heart where dreams belong.
Holding tight to warmth and grace,
In shadows, we find our embrace.

A flicker glows in twilight's breath,
Life thrives beyond the grasp of death.
Each moment etched in velvet night,
Illuminated by love's pure light.

From darkness blooms a tender trust,
In tangled paths where shadows rust.
With every heartbeat, echoes soar,
The keeper's love forevermore.

Through the mist, where silence hides,
In the depth where longing bides.
A symphony of souls entwined,
In shadows, true love we find.

The Secret Flame of the Witching Soul

In the forest, secrets flare,
Witching whispers fill the air.
A flicker of the ancient old,
A flame within, warm and bold.

Night descends with velvet grace,
Mystic echoes, sacred space.
Among the trees, a lantern sighs,
The witching soul never dies.

Potions brewed with whispered dreams,
Starlit paths and silver beams.
The secret flame, it dances bright,
Igniting hearts with soft, warm light.

In shadows cast by moonlit glow,
The embers share what few may know.
A truth unveiled, the fire's role,
Awakens life, the witching soul.

With every spark, a story told,
Of love and loss, of brave and bold.
In whispered spells and ancient scrolls,
The secret flame warms endless souls.

Kings and Queens of Flickering Lore

In a realm where shadows sway,
Kings and queens in grand display.
Flickering tales through time extend,
A woven fate that will not bend.

Crowned in light of embered skies,
Echoes haunt as history flies.
Through ages past, the legends grow,
In every heart, their glories flow.

Once upon a twilight's glen,
Heroes rise and fall again.
With every whisper from the past,
A flickering spark forever lasts.

On thrones of tales, they carry weight,
In woven threads of love and fate.
Every heartbeat, a tale reborn,
The flickering adorns our morn.

Guardians of the stories spun,
In every dusk, their race not run.
Kings and queens, eternally soar,
In flickering lore, forevermore.

Hidden Fires in the Alchemist's Cage

Within the cage, the secrets hide,
Alchemy and dreams collide.
Hidden fires gently blaze,
Transforming life in wondrous ways.

Beneath the surface, magic brews,
Veiled in shadows, a mystic muse.
The potion's glow, a spark ignites,
In alchemist's heart, the future writes.

Elements dance, a sacred art,
Turning lead to gold, the alchemist's heart.
In hidden corners, desires alight,
Crafting wonders from the night.

Chants of ages linger near,
Each element whispers, crystal clear.
In every flask, a world unbound,
Hidden fires wait to be found.

With patience true, the secrets yield,
In the cage, the dreams are sealed.
Unraveled by the daring soul,
Hidden fires make the heart whole.

Glowing Connections in the Night's Embrace

In twilight's cloak, we find our spark,
Whispers woven in the dark.
Hands entwined, hearts align,
In this moment, we are divine.

Stars above, they guide our way,
Through the shadows where we sway.
Dreams ignited, burning bright,
Together we dance in the night.

Echoes soft, they call our name,
In this bond, we twist the frame.
With each laugh, with every sigh,
Our glowing hearts begin to fly.

Fading worries, lost in time,
Here we linger, so sublime.
Breath by breath, we weave our fate,
In the stillness, we create.

Love ignites, a gentle flame,
In this embrace, we're not the same.
With every gaze, we redefine,
Connections made, forever shine.

Fables of the Flickering Barrier

Beyond the edge, where night unfolds,
Fables whispered, secrets told.
In the glow of flickering light,
We cross the boundary, take flight.

Threads of stories intertwine,
Boundless realms, all align.
In shadows deep, we dare to roam,
Finding echoes of our home.

Beneath the stars, our lore takes shape,
Magic woven in every gape.
Each flicker holds a tale untold,
A tapestry of the brave and bold.

Sanctuary in darkened glens,
Where the flickering feeling begins.
Together, we harvest what we find,
A fable formed in heart and mind.

In the night, our stories blaze,
Guided by the flicker's gaze.
With every pulse, we write our own,
In the silence, we're never alone.

The Pursuit of Shadows in Droning Light

Chasing shadows 'neath the glow,
In droning light, time moves slow.
Every flicker, a tale concealed,
Whispers of the past revealed.

Echoes linger, haunting grace,
In every corner, we find our place.
With fleeting steps, we roam the night,
In pursuit of dreams, in endless flight.

Shadows dance under moon's embrace,
Illusions soft as they interlace.
We dive deeper, hearts on fire,
In this realm, we never tire.

Voices call, we heed their sound,
In the rush, new worlds abound.
Each heartbeat, a fleeting tease,
In droning light, we glide with ease.

Cascading hopes and wishes blend,
Finding treasures around each bend.
Through persistence, we claim the night,
In shadows' chase, we feel the light.

Celestial Dreams of Primitive Flames

In the hush of night, we ignite,
Celestial dreams take their flight.
Primitive flames, they spark inside,
Within our hearts, where passions bide.

Astral whispers, soft and clear,
Calling us closer, drawing near.
We dance with stars, wild and free,
In this trance, just you and me.

Fires flicker, shadows play,
Guided by the Milky Way.
In the glow of what we've found,
We chase the dreams that know no bounds.

Time dissolves as we embrace,
Moments linger in space.
With every spark, we blend our souls,
A universe that ignites and rolls.

Primitive hearts, eternal flames,
In celestial realms, love claims names.
Together we soar through endless night,
In our dreams, we find the light.

Phantoms of Ember and Enchantment

In shadows deep where whispers dwell,
Phantoms dance like stories to tell.
With flickering flames that dimly burn,
The heart of night, to them we turn.

Lost echoes of a timeless lore,
They beckon us to seek much more.
Enchanted realms of ancient sight,
Where dreams take flight in the velvet night.

Veils of mist and glowing sighs,
In the ember's glow, mystery lies.
With every step, the air grows thick,
A tapestry woven, both frayed and slick.

Softly they weave through tree and glen,
Where magic stirs beyond the ken.
The phantoms twirl in wild delight,
Enchanting souls in the silver light.

In their embrace, the forgotten yearn,
To join the dance, to twist and turn.
So let us wander where they tread,
In the realm where all is said and read.

Secrets Embers Hide Beneath

In glowing coals, a story sleeps,
Whispers trapped in shadows deep.
Beneath the surface, truths entwine,
In ashes, visions blur and shine.

What secrets lurk in crimson blaze?
Flickering through forgotten days.
Each spark a tale of love and woe,
A flicker of light from ages long ago.

The warmth it holds, yet cold it seems,
A veil of dusk that shrouds our dreams.
In silent longing, we draw near,
To listen close, for heartbeats clear.

Among the embers, shadows play,
Offering glimpses of a past gray.
With every crackle, the spirit sighs,
Unraveling stories from the skies.

So gather 'round and let us seek,
The quiet whispers that the flames speak.
In every ember, a promise keeps,
The secrets that the heart still weeps.

Glow of the Witch's Enclosure

In a haven where the wild winds rest,
The witch's glow shines at her behest.
With herbs and spells, the night is spun,
Under the gaze of the silver sun.

Around her cauldron, shadows weave,
Crafting dreams that none believe.
Elixirs swirl in the midnight air,
Brimming with secrets laid bare.

The warmth envelops with gentle grace,
Inviting all to find their place.
In her domain, the spirits roam,
Finding solace, making it home.

With murmurs soft as the evening haze,
She charms the stars to dance and blaze.
In every flicker, a story unfolds,
Of ancient magic and futures bold.

So step within, and feel the peace,
Where heartache and longing find release.
Embrace the glow, let shadows wane,
In the witch's light, there's no more pain.

Candlelight Treads the Witching Hour

When the clock strikes, and shadows sway,
Candlelight marks the witching way.
In flickers soft, the spirits call,
To dance with echoes in the hall.

A gentle glow fills the midnight air,
Awakening dreams, both bright and rare.
With every flame, a tale ignites,
Painting the world with whispered sights.

The hour of magic, both eerie and bright,
As secrets drift into the night.
Each flame a beacon, guiding lost,
Through realms unseen, they'll pay the cost.

Obsidian shadows, a tapestry spun,
Weaving stories of all that's undone.
In this moment, the past aligns,
As candlelight breathes and softly shines.

Embrace the dark, let silence speak,
As mysteries murmur and spirits peek.
In candlelight's glow, we shall find our way,
Treading softly, through night to day.

Echoes of Flame in the Sorceress's Keep

In the dark of night, whispers rise,
Embers dance beneath starry skies.
Secrets breathe in shadows deep,
Echoes of flame in the sorceress's keep.

Cloaked in mystery, her eyes aglow,
Threads of magic in moonlit flow.
Casting spells with a gentle hand,
Weaving fate in a timeless land.

Chants of power fill the air,
Silent watchers float in despair.
Ancient runes begin to creep,
Echoes of flame in the sorceress's keep.

With every flicker, the past awakes,
In enchanted dreams, the cosmos shakes.
Whispers of courage, binds the weak,
Hidden truths the flames now speak.

As dawn approaches, light shall break,
From the starlit realms, choices to make.
Within her heart, a promise deep,
Echoes of flame in the sorceress's keep.

Reflections Between Gloom and Radiance

Shadows stretch where whispers dwell,
Beneath the veil, a forgotten spell.
Light and dark in a tender dance,
Reflections held in fate's expanse.

Glimmers spark in the heavy haze,
Twilight flickers, a subtle blaze.
Nights that linger, hopes entwine,
Between the gloom, the stars align.

Through silent woods, an echo flows,
Veiled in silver, the memory grows.
In the mirror of the soul, we seek,
Reflections drawn from the light we peak.

Moments fade like morning mist,
In the balance, the heart cannot resist.
Guided gently on paths unique,
Reflections breathe where shadows speak.

In the final glimmer of the night,
The dawn will rise, reclaim its light.
Hope will carry the soul's mystique,
Reflections blending in radiant peak.

Enchantments of the Flickering Prism

Colors swirl in a cosmic dance,
Fragments glimmer, fate's romance.
In the heart of night, dreams take flight,
Enchantments weave with soft twilight.

Each hue whispers secrets untold,
Spectrum's magic in the bold.
A flickering prism, shadows play,
Bringing forth night, banishing day.

As stars align in silent grace,
Illuminated in this sacred place.
Captured visions in every beam,
Enchantments spark with a silent gleam.

Through every shimmer, a echo sings,
Ancient lore of forgotten things.
In twilight's caress, we find the key,
Enchantments unfold in eternity.

In tranquil moments, stillness reigns,
And beauty flows through energy chains.
Guided by light, our spirits glean,
Enchantments bloom in colors unseen.

The Witch's Heart in Twilight Light

Beyond the woods, where shadows throng,
The witch's heart beats, wild and strong.
Pulsing gently, a flame so bright,
In the embrace of twilight light.

Whispers linger in the cooling air,
Mystical paths lead beyond despair.
With secrets held in ancient rite,
The witch's heart glows, an ethereal sight.

Through tangled vines, her magic flows,
A potent force that never slows.
Crimson dreams and moonlit flight,
The witch's heart in shimmering sight.

Echoes of laughter blend with sighs,
A dance of time beneath the skies.
In every spell, there's love's delight,
The witch's heart ignites the night.

As stars awaken, shadows shift,
With every heartbeat, the spirit lifts.
In twilight's glow, truths reunite,
The witch's heart in endless light.

Mysteries of the Shadowed Hearth

In the corner where shadows dwell,
Secrets linger, stories to tell.
Softly crackles the ancient wood,
Holding dreams of the forgotten good.

Beneath a cloak of ember light,
Memories dance, lost to the night.
A whispered tale of love and loss,
The hearth bears witness, a silent gloss.

Shadows flicker, spirits drawn near,
In the warmth, they shed their fear.
Echoes entwined in the smoke's embrace,
Time stands still in this sacred space.

Gather 'round the gentle flame,
Hearts ignite, yet none are the same.
Sparks of laughter, tears, and lore,
Binding the past forevermore.

Crackling flames reveal the past,
Woven tales that forever last.
In the hearth's glow, life's truths unfold,
Mysteries written in embers bold.

Flickers in the Enchanted Grimoire

Pages turn with a gentle sigh,
Whispers echo from days gone by.
Flickers of magic light the way,
In the grimoire where spirits play.

In ink and dust, the power lies,
Chants and spells beneath the skies.
Each word woven with care and thought,
In every verse, a battle fought.

Underneath the twilight's dome,
Incantations find their home.
Mystical runes that softly gleam,
Guide the heart into a dream.

Holding wonder within the page,
Ancient secrets for every age.
A flicker shown in candle's glow,
Unlocking doors we long to know.

The grimoire sings in midnight's breath,
Calling forth from beyond the death.
With every flicker, desire grows,
In enchanted light, a path bestows.

The Luminous Secrets of the Spellbound

In the night where enchantment thrives,
Luminous secrets twirl, and jive.
Magic whispers in the cool air,
Promises of wonders fair.

Lights that flicker, dance, and play,
Show the hidden realms, they say.
Each secret held within the heart,
A spellbinding journey, a brand new start.

Stars awaken with tales to weave,
In the glow, we choose to believe.
Bound by the light, the mystic dream,
Nothing is ever as it seems.

Through the shadows, the luminous forms,
Guide the seeker in mystical storms.
A world unveiled in twilight's grace,
Filled with wonders we long to chase.

Spellbound by the luminous might,
Lost in the fabric of the night.
Each secret bright, a guide to find,
The magic waiting for hearts aligned.

Whispers of the Embered Witchcraft

Beneath the moon's watchful eye,
Ember whispers softly sigh.
Witching hour brings forth the flame,
Secrets spoken, none the same.

In the shadows, potions brew,
Crafting magic old and new.
With each flicker, spells take flight,
Guided by the starry night.

Echoes drift on sultry breeze,
Through the trees, a whispered tease.
Witchcraft woven in amber threads,
Dreams ignited, as daylight sheds.

Ancient runes in circle drawn,
Understood as dusk greets dawn.
Each ember holds a spirit's song,
In the glow, we all belong.

Whispers linger, secrets thrive,
In the hearth, our souls arrive.
Ember witchcraft will unveil,
Magic timeless, love's true trail.

Illuminated Echoes of a Forgotten Spell

Whispers dance in the twilight air,
Echoes lost, a time laid bare.
Memories woven in shadows deep,
Guarding secrets that the night will keep.

Glowing runes on ancient stone,
Tell stories of a world once known.
Flickering flames in the moon's embrace,
Illuminate the forgotten space.

A sorcerer's sigh, a lover's plea,
Breezes carry spells like a gentle sea.
Through the silence, magic flows,
Binding hearts where the moonlight glows.

Silent witnesses of yesteryear,
In the stillness, we hold them near.
Ethereal light, a shimmering thread,
Tracks the journeys of the unspoken dead.

As dusk falls, secrets unfurl,
In the shadows of a dreamlike swirl.
With each pulse, the past reclaims,
In illuminated echoes, we find our names.

Twisted Flames in the Circle of Secrets

In the hearth, shadows twist and turn,
Secrets smolder, waiting to burn.
Dancing embers, a silent call,
In the circle, we rise or fall.

Flickers of truth beneath the lies,
Silhouettes whispering soft goodbyes.
Beneath the glow, hearts intertwine,
As twisted flames reveal the design.

Veils of smoke, a cryptic sign,
Revealing tales of the divine.
With each spark, a story grows,
In the circle, the magic flows.

Ancient echoes from the fire's breath,
In the dance, they speak of death.
Yet life ignites in fragile splendor,
Twisted flames, forever tender.

As night descends, the whispers rise,
Secrets hidden from worldly eyes.
In the circle, all truths collide,
Twisted flames cannot be denied.

Secrets Illuminated by Night's Guardian

Beneath the stars, the night holds sway,
Guarding secrets in shadows at play.
With every beat, hearts softly sigh,
Illuminated dreams that never die.

A silver glow from the moonlit sky,
Reveals the path where lost souls fly.
Whispers echo in a cosmic dance,
Inviting souls to seize their chance.

Once hidden truths come softly forth,
Guided by the night's gentle worth.
In the silence, clarity breaks,
Where shadows linger, a new hope wakes.

Embraced by the dark, fears disappear,
Night's guardian draws us near.
With zephyrs sweet and starlit grace,
We discover our forgotten place.

Enshrined in the twilight, promises bloom,
Beneath the stars, dispelling gloom.
Together we weave through the endless night,
Secrets illuminated, burning bright.

Bewitched Glow Through Gilded Bars

In a cage of gold, the silence weeps,
Where dreams linger, and memory keeps.
A haunted glow from within the bars,
Whispers secrets like fallen stars.

The moonlight trickles through the steel,
Enchanting shadows, what they conceal.
With every flicker, a tale unfolds,
Of longing hearts and destinies bold.

Gilded dreams held tight in chains,
The heart beats on, though freedom wanes.
In the depths of night, hope finds a way,
To break the dawn of a brighter day.

Each moment bathed in ethereal light,
Dreams and wishes take to flight.
From bars of gold, the spirit soars,
Into the realms beyond those doors.

With haunted glow, the cage transforms,
Into a beacon amidst the storms.
Love's enchantment fills the air,
In bewitched glow, we find our care.

Alchemy of Flame and Enchantment

In shadows deep where whispers dance,
The flicker warms a fleeting glance.
With every spark, a secret weaves,
In the heart, the magic breathes.

Embers rise like dreams untold,
Transforming pain into pure gold.
Each swirl of fire, a tale reborn,
From ashes new, the night is worn.

An alchemist's hand begins to trace,
The patterns bright, a sacred space.
With intertwined fates that gently spark,
The flame ignites a revel's arc.

In every blaze, a passion ignites,
Through every shadow, pure delight.
The dance of fate unfolds so grand,
Where every heart and flame withstand.

So heed the night, let flames entwine,
For in their glow, the stars align.
With echoes soft of ancient songs,
The alchemy of flames belongs.

Lanterns of Enigma in the Dark

Beneath the veil of moonlit grace,
Lanterns flicker, a strange embrace.
They guide the lost with gentle beams,
Illuminating forgotten dreams.

Each lantern holds a tale apart,
A flick of hope within the heart.
The whispers weave through twisted nights,
As shadows dance in fleeting lights.

In darkness deep, where secrets play,
These glowing orbs lead souls astray.
The paths are winding, shrouded, wide,
Yet within their glow, we find our guide.

The enigma rises, soft yet bold,
Each flame a story waiting told.
In silent nights, their purpose clear,
To anchor dreams, to draw us near.

So take a breath, and trust the light,
For lanterns spark within the night.
With every step, the world will bloom,
In the dance of shadows, we find room.

Celestial Glow Amidst Forbidden Rituals

Under starlit, sacred skies,
A celestial glow begins to rise.
In whispers lost, the night unfolds,
As ancient secrets dare be told.

Forbidden rites in shadows blend,
Where time suspends and dreams transcend.
The glowing haze of twilight's grace,
Draws forth the brave to seek their place.

With candles lit in circle wide,
The spirits gather, none to hide.
An echo stirs, a dance begun,
In celestial light, we are as one.

Amongst the stars, the rituals sway,
As magic intertwines, come what may.
The moon's embrace, a guiding hand,
In the heart's core, we understand.

So let us journey, deep and far,
In the glow of our ancient star.
With spirits high, we will not fall,
For in these rites, we summon all.

Flickers of Fate in the Sorcery's Hold

In twilight's grip, the air grows thick,
Flickers of fate in shadows stick.
The sorcery's hold, a spellbound trance,
Where destinies whirl in wild dance.

With every flicker, a choice is made,
As time unfolds, the game is played.
Each spark, a whisper of what could be,
In the sorcerer's gaze, the world can see.

Threads of magic weave us near,
In every heartbeat, we're intertwined here.
The flickers taunt, yet they guide,
Through darkened lanes where secrets hide.

Each moment glistens, bright and rare,
In the tapestry spun from starlit air.
With courage drawn, we face the night,
For in our hands, we wield the light.

So let the shadows play their part,
As we embark with boundless heart.
In the sorcery's grip, we will find our way,
For fate's true dance is ours to sway.

Beneath the Witching Glow of Night's Caress

In the hush of midnight's breath,
Stars shimmer like whispered secrets,
Moonbeams dance on velvet skies,
While shadows weave their ancient tales.

Crickets serenade the dark,
As trees sway with mystic grace,
A chill wraps around the heart,
Inviting whispers from the past.

Ghostly figures roam the woods,
Embers flicker in their wake,
The air thick with untold dreams,
Moments lost to time's cruel flow.

Beneath the vibrant painted skies,
Magic lingers on each breeze,
Every sigh a story shared,
In this realm of moonlit spells.

The Flicker that Guides the Lost Souls

In the depths of twilight's sigh,
Flickering flames reveal their path,
Glow like beacons in the night,
Drawing wanderers from the dark.

Safeguards for the weary souls,
Casting warmth amidst the chill,
Glimmers of forgotten dreams,
Each spark a tale of long ago.

Amidst the shadows walked they,
Searching for the light within,
Every flicker tells a story,
Hopes rekindled in the glow.

Voices echo on the breeze,
Guiding hearts that seek their way,
Through the mazes of despair,
Faith ignites in night's embrace.

Chronicles of the Enchanted Embers

Upon the hearth where tales are spun,
Embers flicker, stories bloom,
Every spark a memory born,
Crackling softly in the gloom.

Legends whisper 'round the fire,
As shadows dance on ancient stone,
Dreamers weave their wistful hopes,
In the glow, they feel at home.

Time lays rest upon each spark,
Igniting visions from the past,
Every flicker a history,
Boundless tales in shadows cast.

Chronicles of joy and fear,
Echoes of the days gone by,
In the warmth of glowing embers,
Hearts find peace in whispered sighs.

Flickering Shadows in the Enchanted Gloom

Shadows flicker, softly sway,
In the hush of twilight's breath,
Mysteries in every curve,
Hints of magic linger near.

Beneath the branches thick and wide,
Figures dance in soft embrace,
Stories spun through moonlit hours,
Voices lost in nature's grace.

Glimmers sparkle on the ground,
Guides for souls who roam alone,
In this realm of whispered dreams,
They find solace in the night.

A tapestry of light and shade,
Woven deep in twilight's heart,
Flickering shadows signify,
The magic in the dark unfolds.

Delicate Threads of Ethereal Flame

In the twilight's soft embrace,
Fleeting whispers dance and twirl,
Threads of fire softly trace,
A tapestry of dreams unfurl.

Each flicker paints a story bright,
Carried on the night's cool breath,
Illuminating shadows' flight,
In the starlit veil of death.

Veils of silk and strands of gold,
Woven by a master hand,
A tale of secrets yet untold,
In this enchanted, glowing land.

Gentle warmth against the chill,
Sparks that pierce the heart of night,
Feeding hopes, igniting will,
In a dance of purest light.

So we stand, united here,
Bound by threads of fate and flame,
With every laugh, and every tear,
We kindle life in love's own name.

Lightborn Mysteries of the Enchanted Cage

In a chamber thick with dreams,
Shadows whisper secrets low,
Born of light, serene it seems,
Mysteries begin to flow.

Caged within these walls of time,
Sparkling hopes in corners hide,
A silent, echoing rhyme,
Where the ancient secrets bide.

Each moment glimmers like a star,
A reflection of the past,
In this realm, we wander far,
In visions that are meant to last.

Enchanted through the twilight's gaze,
Awakening of inner sights,
The heart's rhythm sets the phase,
For the dawn of endless nights.

As we weave the tales of light,
Beneath the cage's silver shell,
We unfold our souls, take flight,
In the spells of stories we tell.

Revelations from Enchanted Shadows

In the hush of midnight's glow,
Shadows weave their ancient lore,
A dance of secrets set to flow,
Whispers echo evermore.

Branches sway with gentle grace,
In the moonlight's tender beam,
Revealing truths we must embrace,
As we chase the fleeting dream.

Ink-stained skies and silken air,
Carved in whispers, soft and deep,
Each confession, unaware,
Unraveling while we quietly sleep.

Ghostly echoes linger still,
Threads of fate intertwining tight,
In the air, a potent thrill,
Wrapped in shadows' cloaked delight.

As dawn breaks, the truth unveiled,
A tapestry of dark and light,
In these moments, hearts have sailed,
To find their home beyond the night.

Bedtime Stories of Outlawed Light

In the hush before the dark,
Where dreams begin to take their flight,
Outlaws tread with whispered spark,
Spinning tales of hidden light.

Once upon a starry eve,
A flicker danced behind closed eyes,
Promises that we believe,
Beneath the vast and watchful skies.

Every shadow holds a spark,
Stories woven in the night,
By the glow, we leave a mark,
In a world that feels so right.

With each tale, a spirit soars,
Boundless as the dreams they hold,
We escape through secret doors,
In the warmth of stories bold.

So close your eyes, come take my hand,
Together let our spirits roam,
In a realm where dreams expand,
As we return to our heart's home.

Shadows Dance Amidst the Arcane Glow

In the twilight, shadows creep,
Whispers echo, secrets deep.
Moonlight spills on ancient stone,
Mysteries held, forever unknown.

Figures waltz in gentle trance,
Haunting beauty, a spectral dance.
Flickering flames, soft and low,
Guiding paths where shadows flow.

Veils of night, they softly sway,
In the midst of dusk's ballet.
Winds of magic weave and spin,
Tales of worlds that lie within.

With each step, the memories twine,
Interwoven, dark, divine.
In the chill, a sigh escapes,
As the night in silence drapes.

Beneath the stars, secrets lay,
In shadows' grasp, they softly play.
A tapestry of dreams unfurl,
In the heart of this strange world.

The Enigma of the Glimmering Smoke

In the fog, a shimmer glows,
A riddle veiled in soft repose.
Swirls of mist, they dance and twirl,
Secrets whispered in a world.

Amber light, the shadows blend,
Curiosity, a curious friend.
Glimmers tease the cautious eye,
With every breath, the truth drifts by.

Ethereal forms begin to rise,
Veiled in words, in soft disguise.
Luring hearts to seek and roam,
The enigma of unknown home.

Fragrant dreams curl in the air,
In the stillness, whispers glare.
Chasing wisps of ancient lore,
Through curves of smoke, forevermore.

Each inhale a story told,
A mystic realm of dreams unfold.
As shadows twine with fleeting light,
In the dance of day and night.

A Haven of Light in Darkest Magic

A flicker glows in the abyss,
Whispers of hope, a gentle kiss.
In the dark, the lantern swings,
Illuminating fragile things.

Where shadows loom, a refuge grows,
Warmth defies the chilling throes.
Hearts, once lost, now find their way,
In the haven, light shall stay.

Veils of darkness ebb and fade,
In the light, no fear is made.
Glimmers chase the dread away,
As dawn emerges, bright and gay.

Through the silence, echoes break,
In the haven, hearts awake.
A sanctuary built on grace,
Cradled in love's warm embrace.

With starlit dreams, we weave our fate,
A tapestry that won't abate.
In darkest magic, light shines clear,
A beacon bright, forever near.

Drifting Light in the Witching Realm

In the shadows where spirits glide,
A drifting light, a willing guide.
Through the veil, soft voices call,
Echoing secrets, rise and fall.

Moonlit trails where phantoms play,
Mysterious paths that lead astray.
Winding whispers, tales replete,
In the hush, the heart will beat.

Floating softly, the lanterns sway,
Glowing embers lead the way.
Lost in wonder, time stands still,
In the realm of magic's thrill.

Every flicker tells a tale,
Of destiny that won't derail.
Guided by the gentle beams,
Awakening the deepest dreams.

As night unfolds its velvet cloak,
Within the light, the shadows spoke.
In this realm where dreams unfurl,
The dancing light spins the world.

Spellbound Firelight's Embrace

In the flicker of flames, a dance does begin,
Whispers of secrets, the night wraps us thin.
Each ember a story, each spark a delight,
Bound in the magic of fire's warm light.

Shadows twist softly, caressing the trees,
As laughter erupts on the cool evening breeze.
We gather like moths, enchanted and free,
Lost in the warmth, just the fire and we.

The stars peek in, wearing crowns of gold,
While hearts beat in rhythm, brave and bold.
In this sacred space, where dreams intertwine,
Firelight reveals what the dark can't confine.

Time drips like wax, the moments we seize,
Each chuckle, each glance, feels like a tease.
Yet here we will linger, till night's gently fades,
In the spell of the fire, our worries cascades.

So let us embrace this ephemeral glow,
Lost in the warmth, surrendered to flow.
For in the firelight, true warmth we find,
A spellbound connection, soul intertwined.

Refuge of Shadows and Glows

Beneath the dark sky, where secrets reside,
A refuge of shadows, where dreams can abide.
The glows of the twilight beckon us near,
Embracing the stillness, our purpose is clear.

In the hush of the night, whispers take flight,
We wander through echoes, where day meets the night.
Each corner a promise, each breath feels alive,
In the realm of the shadows, our spirits revive.

Here lies the comfort, a gentle caress,
Shrouded in mystery, we fearlessly press.
The dance of the night, like a silken thread,
Weaving through hearts that once wandered and fled.

In this hidden embrace, we find our way home,
Where the interplay glimmers, like seeds in the loam.
The shadows, they cradle, the glows intertwine,
A haven for souls, where destinies align.

So come take my hand, let the darkness unfold,
This refuge we've found, where we break the mold.
Together we'll wander, where light meets the grey,
In shadows and glows, we shall forever stay.

Dancers Behind the Witch's Veil

Under the moonlight, a secret revealed,
With whispers of magic, the heart is unsealed.
The dancers emerge, from shadows they weave,
Behind the witch's veil, tales we believe.

Silken threads twirl in the cool midnight air,
Mysteries linger, with a touch of flair.
They beckon the night, with laughter and grace,
Invisibility cloaks, yet their passion's embraced.

In spells of enchantment, they twine and they spin,
With echoes of secrets, the stories begin.
A flicker of fire, a sudden spark bright,
Dancers unite under the cloak of the night.

Each step a whisper, each glance a caress,
A rhythm of hearts, in the moon's soft finesse.
The veil sways with magic, both dark and divine,
Eclipsing the world, where shadows entwine.

So linger with me, in this mystic embrace,
Let whispers of wonder play slow in our pace.
For behind the witch's veil, we'll dance through the spell,

In a world of enchantment, where all is well.

Light's Shadowed Embrace in the Enchantment

In whispers of twilight, where shadows convene,
The light dances gently, in hues so serene.
An embrace of enchantment, where shadows reside,
In the gentle caress, our spirits collide.

The air is electric, with magic untold,
As starlight weaves softly, in threads of pure gold.
Each flicker a promise, a heartbeat anew,
In the light's shadowed embrace, we find our truth.

Through gardens of starlight, we wander so free,
With echoes of laughter, nostalgia's decree.
The fairies take flight, on whispers we soar,
With joy in our hearts, we yearn for much more.

This temple of twilight, a sacred retreat,
Where shadows and light weave their magic discreet.
In the arms of the night, we twirl and we sway,
Finding solace and strength, come what may.

So let us embrace this dance, bold and true,
In the light's shadowed embrace, it's me and you.
For in this enchantment, we rise and we gleam,
Together forever, a beautifully shared dream.

Whispers of Light Within Arcane Chambers

In corners dim where secrets dwell,
A flicker glows, a soft sweet spell.
Echoes dance on ancient stone,
In silence wrapped, we're not alone.

The books of lore, their pages turn,
With whispered dreams, our hearts will burn.
A magic woven in the air,
Draws us close, with silent care.

Within these walls, the shadows creep,
Guarding truths that we must keep.
Through every crack, the light will pour,
Illuminating what's before.

A promise made in twilight's breath,
Awakens hope, defying death.
As tales of old entwine with night,
We find our purpose in the light.

In arcane chambers, whispers flow,
Guiding us where few may go.
With every step, the magic swells,
In whispered tones, the heart compels.

The Lure of Flicker in Twilight's Hold

In twilight's breath, the shadows sway,
A dance of light, both bold and fey.
Colors bleed on horizons wide,
Nights embrace, where dreams abide.

The flicker lures like distant stars,
Through whispered paths and silver spars.
Echoing softly, the secrets told,
In twilight's grip, we grow so bold.

Each moment holds a fleeting chance,
To waltz within the shadows' dance.
The world unfolds, a painter's brush,
In every heartbeat, feel the rush.

A flame ignites, igniting the skies,
While night unveils its deep disguise.
With every flicker, the darkness fades,
In twilight's hold, our hope cascades.

Captured whispers in the quiet hush,
A gentle touch, a sudden rush.
In every glow, the heart finds peace,
As twilight plays, and dreams release.

Shadows Breathing in the Warlock's Lair

In the depths where shadows breathe,
Mysteries hide, we must retrieve.
The warlock's lair, a realm of night,
Where echoes pulse with haunting light.

Candles flicker, casting fears,
In whispers soft, the truth appears.
Darkened corners speak of fate,
Awaken dreams we contemplate.

Spells entwine in spectral streams,
Treading softly on our dreams.
The air is thick with ancient lore,
Within these walls, we crave for more.

A chessboard laid, each piece is set,
In shadowed games, we won't forget.
A warlock's hand, a puppet's sway,
In this dance of dark and play.

With every breath, the night unfolds,
As shadows weave their tales of bolds.
In this lair, we find our threads,
In quiet whispers and ancient beds.

Captured Fire and Bewitching Glimmer

From captured fire, the embers glow,
A bewitching warmth, we come to know.
In every spark, a tale ignites,
Of hidden dreams on starry nights.

Glimmers dance in the velvet dark,
Lighting paths, each one a spark.
Spinning tales of what may be,
In shadows cast, we learn to see.

With every flicker, hearts entwine,
In fiery circles, we transcend time.
Through whispered chants, the night returns,
For captured fire forever burns.

Memories weave in the woven glow,
Each shimmering light, a soft hello.
Entwined we stand in tranquil bliss,
A dance with fate, a gentle kiss.

Bewitching glimmer, a secret share,
In wild hearts, we rise, we dare.
A taste of magic in every breath,
In captured fire, we've found our path.

Secrets Beyond the Flame's Boundary

In the hearth, whispers creep,
Secrets old and secrets deep.
Flickering shadows dance and play,
Guarding tales of night and day.

Embers glow with stories spun,
Of battles lost and victories won.
Flames caress the air so light,
Revealing truths hidden from sight.

Lost souls seek a warming spark,
Lighting paths within the dark.
Through the smoke, they yearn for peace,
Finding solace, sweet release.

Voices echo, soft yet clear,
Promises and hidden fear.
Beyond the flame, the heart will yearn,
For knowledge gained and lessons learned.

In the flicker, a truth shines bold,
Stories woven, ancient and told.
Secrets linger, forever near,
Beyond the flame, they reappear.

Dance of Shadows within the Celestial Fright

In the night sky, shadows sway,
Dancing where the lost dreams lay.
Stars twinkle with an eerie light,
Veiling fears of the endless night.

Winds whisper secrets of the unseen,
Haunting figures fill the serene.
As planets spin in cosmic waltz,
The universe reveals its faults.

In the dark, a crescent moon,
Guides the dancers, frail and strewn.
With each step, a story told,
Of forgotten loves and glories bold.

Through the veil, a flicker glows,
Illuminating where no warmth goes.
In the gloom, they seek a sign,
A promise etched in the divine.

Galaxies hum a spectral tune,
Embracing shadows, cradling the moon.
And as they sway, the world holds its breath,
In the dance of shadows, life and death.

Sources of Light in the Witch's Sanctum

In the heart of the old stone tower,
Lies a mystery cloaked in power.
Candles flicker, their glow so bright,
Drawing forth the hidden light.

Herbs hang dry from beams above,
Whispers of the earth, a magic love.
With every potion brewed with care,
The essence of life fills the air.

Crystals sparkle, a prismed play,
Channeling wishes in their own way.
Each facet tells a tale untold,
Of dreams that shimmer and hearts that hold.

The cauldron bubbles, secrets spin,
Magic stirs, inviting in.
With every turn, the future bends,
Transcending time, weaving trends.

In shadows cast by candle's grace,
Wisdom dwells in this sacred space.
Sources of light in dark's embrace,
Guarding spells with boundless pace.

Softly Glowing Edges of Dark Arts

Beneath the veil of midnight's call,
Quiet whispers rise and fall.
Edges glow where shadows play,
In the realm where spirits sway.

Darkness yields to a subtle light,
Painting hues in the still of night.
Casting spells with fingers deft,
Transforming all that was once left.

In the corners where secrets dwell,
Mysteries weave a magic spell.
With every breath, the air grows thick,
As shadows dance, swift and slick.

Glimmers flicker, shaping fear,
Carving paths that draw us near.
In the silence, echoes fade,
Softly glowing, the dark arts made.

With murmured chants, the energy swells,
In the depths where enchantment dwells.
From edges drawn, a story starts,
In softly glowing, darkened arts.

Ethereal Light in the Sorceress's Grasp

In twilight's gentle sigh, she weaves,
Threads of silver and moonlit leaves.
Whispers dance around her spell,
Casting secrets, all is well.

Her fingers trace the glowing air,
With every spark, the shadows flare.
Mystery sings in her command,
A realm created by her hand.

Stars awaken at her call,
A cosmic echo in the hall.
Illumined dreams take flight at dawn,
In her realm, the night is drawn.

The world bends to her will's embrace,
In the light, we find our place.
Ethereal whispers, bright and bold,
In her grasp, the tales unfold.

A dance beneath the silver sky,
Where hopes and wishes learn to fly.
Light entwined with shadows cast,
In every moment, magic lasts.

Mystical Luminescence Behind Iron Bars

In a cage of rust, the light persists,
Dancing shadows, tender twists.
Behind cold iron, glimmers shine,
Whispers of hope, a sacred sign.

Flickers breathe where darkness lies,
A hopeful glow that never dies.
Silent secrets, the night confesses,
In the gloom, the spirit blesses.

Through barred windows, magic streams,
Life awakens within dreams.
Each ray a promise, softly spun,
In quiet moments, battles won.

The heart beats on, unbroken, free,
In the shadows, a symphony.
Mystical luminescence calls,
Bringing life to ancient walls.

In the silence, courage grows,
A luminous path that softly glows.
Beyond the bars, the world expands,
Where light and shadows join their hands.

Echoes of Glow in the Witch's Sanctuary

In the haven of herbs and spells,
Where quiet magic gently dwells.
Echoes of glow in every nook,
Secrets penned in an old, worn book.

Candles flicker, a soft embrace,
Illuminating her sacred space.
Whispers travel on the air,
Each note a spell, a loving prayer.

Crimson threads and midnight tones,
Mingle with the ancient stones.
Nature's power, hers to wield,
In the sanctuary, dreams are healed.

Her laughter rings like silver chimes,
A melody that bridges times.
Echoes dance in moonlit streams,
Reflecting all her hidden dreams.

Bathed in light, the potions brew,
Creating life from fading dew.
In every corner, magic flows,
In the witch's heart, the garden grows.

The Dance of Shadows in a Celestial Prison

In twilight's arms, the shadows sway,
A cosmic ballet, lost in play.
Stars whisper secrets in the night,
As darkness waltzes with the light.

Celestial chains hold dreams at bay,
Yet in this void, the spirits stay.
Each flicker of hope ignites the air,
In whispered echoes, they declare.

The moon reveals the truth within,
As shadowed forms begin to spin.
Held in orbit, yet so alive,
In every heart, the will to thrive.

Tendrils of light weave through the dark,
Where every flicker leaves a mark.
In this prison, creation flows,
A dance of shadows before it glows.

Celestial beings, trapped yet free,
Blending boundaries of reality.
In the night, they find their bliss,
In eternal dance, an endless kiss.

Gentle Flicker Among Darkened Runes

In shadows deep, a candle's light,
Whispers of magic take their flight.
Runes aglow, secrets unfold,
As night embraces tales untold.

The air is thick with ancient charms,
Echoing softly, the night alarms.
Flickering bright, the flame shall weave,
Mysteries born of what we believe.

Each rune sparked, a story to share,
Of lost realms and dreams laid bare.
The dance of shadows, ethereal grace,
A gentle flicker, a sacred space.

With every breath, the darkness stirs,
Boundless whispers, the heart concurs.
In flicker's glow, old tales resound,
Lost to the ages, now newly found.

Embracing night, the runes awake,
In the hush, our dreams partake.
With gentle flickers, we seek the truth,
Among darkened runes, we reclaim our youth.

Rituals Illuminated in the Witch's Lair

Moonlit shadows cast their spell,
In the lair where secrets dwell.
Chants and whispers, softly spoken,
Rituals of power, unbroken.

Candles flicker against the stone,
Symbols drawn, the world untone.
In the circle, the magic swirls,
As the witch weaves her mystic pearls.

Herbs entwined, a fragrant blend,
Through the night, the spirits send.
With every beat of the heart's embrace,
Rituals dance in timeless grace.

Incense rises, curling high,
Connecting earth and the starry sky.
The cauldron bubbles, secrets brew,
In the witch's lair, all feels true.

As moonlight spills through cracks in stone,
Crafting dreams where shadows moan.
At her hands, the night ignites,
Rituals bloom in fire-light sights.

Hues of Fire in a Forgotten Celestial

In the vastness, colors collide,
Hues of fire where darkness hides.
Stars twinkle in a silent waltz,
A dance of dreams, the cosmos' pulse.

Galaxies swirl, painted bright,
Whispers of ages lost to night.
A celestial canvas, vibrant and grand,
Light years away, yet close at hand.

In this space, secrets ignite,
Flames of passion, pure delight.
Fragments of time, gently they sway,
Where hues of fire lead the way.

Constellations speak in hues divine,
Tales of love and loss entwined.
In the silence, fierce and clear,
Celestial echoes, all we hold dear.

A tapestry woven with fiery threads,
Each color a memory, briefly spreads.
In the night sky's embrace, we find,
Hues of fire, eternal, intertwined.

Emblems Embedded in Soft Glows

In twilight's grasp, soft glows arise,
Emblems crafted from starry skies.
Glimmers subtle, a tender dance,
Mysteries emerge, given a chance.

Each emblem whispers tales profound,
Of forgotten worlds, lost and found.
Through subtle hues, their stories weave,
In soft glows, we learn to believe.

Patterns etched in shimmering light,
Guiding the wanderer through the night.
In their presence, shadows retreat,
A warmth embraced, tender and sweet.

The air is rich with dreams once sung,
In the silence, hearts are strung.
Soft glows linger, wisdom to share,
Emblems waiting, a tranquil flare.

With every flicker, hope ignites,
In the silence of the night's delights.
Embedded deep in our souls, they flow,
Emblems cherished, in soft glows.

Secrets of the Conjurer's Lantern

In shadows deep the lantern glows,
Its whispers weave through night's repose.
With flickering light, it tells its tales,
Of ancient arts and mystic gales.

A flick of wrist, a whispered name,
And secrets dance, igniting flame.
The air thickens, a velvet shroud,
As dreams of sorcery swell and crowd.

A conjurer's heart beats soft and shy,
While visions shimmer, spirits nigh.
Each glimmer holds a path untold,
In radiant hues, the magic unfolds.

Within its glow, time often bends,
Connecting worlds, where fate transcends.
A spark of truth, a flash of art,
The lantern's pulse ignites the heart.

So heed the call, embrace the night,
Where every shadow finds its light.
For in this world of unseen ties,
The conjurer's magic never dies.

The Embrace of Wax and Whisper

Beneath the moon, the candles weep,
With secrets kept, a promise steep.
In pools of wax, the shadows creep,
While whispered dreams through silence seep.

The flicker dances, a lover's tease,
As time suspends upon the breeze.
In melting warmth, our souls unite,
Entwined in shades of soft twilight.

Each whispered word, a tender touch,
In the quiet night, we give so much.
The scent of lore fills up the air,
As hearts conjoin in whispered prayer.

A tapestry of warmth and glow,
In every sigh, the candles know.
The embrace of wax, a lasting plea,
In this cocoon, just you and me.

With every flicker, let love shine,
In melted dreams, your heart is mine.
Together bound in flickering flight,
In the embrace of wax tonight.

Caged Flames of Arcane Dreams

Behind the bars, the embers flare,
In a shadowed cage, they dance and dare.
These flames confined, yet wild they roam,
In a realm where dreams have found their home.

With each soft crackle, a story brews,
Of ancient spells and cosmic hues.
The caged flames pulse with fervent might,
Illuminating the endless night.

Bound by fate, yet longing to fly,
With whispered wishes printed in the sky.
Arcane visions stir within their glow,
A flicker of hope in shadows below.

In quiet corners, a power burns bright,
Potential alive in waning night.
For every spark, a dream awakes,
In the ember's grasp, our future takes.

So tend the flames, let visions bloom,
In the caged heart of darkness loom.
With courage vast, let spirits gleam,
And unleash the caged flames of dreams.

Gleaming Spheres in a Woven Spell

In twilight's grip, the spheres align,
Crafted from threads of fate divine.
With colors bright, they twirl and spin,
Invoking magic that dwells within.

In every orb, a story swells,
An aura bursts, where wonder dwells.
A woven spell of joy and fear,
In every glance, the cosmos near.

Beneath the stars, the dancers sway,
As moonlight chases shadows away.
In rhythms soft, enchantments weave,
Unfolding layers we can't perceive.

Each sphere a promise, bright and true,
A glimmering path our hearts pursue.
Through woven dreams, we seek and find,
The echoes of an ancient mind.

So hold them close, these radiant spheres,
In every glance, release your fears.
For in their light, we see our fate,
A woven spell to celebrate.

Charm of the Enchanted Illumination

In twilight's soft embrace we find,
Stars whisper secrets, nights unwind.
Moonbeams dance on leaves so green,
A world awakens, bright and keen.

With each flicker, shadows sway,
Mystery unfolds, guiding our way.
In every corner, magic weaves,
Reality's flight, the heart believes.

A gentle breeze hums ancient tunes,
Carrying dreams beneath the moons.
Pathways glimmer, a radiant glow,
Leading us where enchantments flow.

Glimmers spark in the cool night air,
Inviting souls that dare to share.
Together we wander, hearts in sync,
Through the light, we pause and think.

In this realm where wonders blend,
Every moment, our spirits mend.
Charm of the night, forever stays,
Illuminating love's soft rays.

Woven Flickers of the Sorcery

Through twisted branches, light breaks free,
Casting spells by the old oak tree.
Each flicker woven, threads of fate,
Binding our hearts, it's never late.

In shadows deep, the sorcery grows,
Whispers of magic, like murmured prose.
Every glimmer tells a tale anew,
Secrets unfold as the night passes through.

With every heartbeat, whispers align,
Woven stories, love's own design.
A dance of flickers, a joyous play,
Enchanting souls in a world of gray.

In hidden realms, the fire ignites,
Breathing warmth into lonely nights.
Woven flickers, enchanting dance,
Inviting all to take a chance.

Together we wander under stars,
Healing wounds, no more scars.
In this magic, we find our way,
Woven flickers lead, come what may.

Enchanted Flames Behind Barred Dreams

In shadows cast by the moon's soft gleam,
Lie the whispers of an unspoken dream.
Enchanted flames that flicker and thrive,
Behind the bars where hopes come alive.

In silence burnt, our passions ignite,
Breaking the chains that kept us from flight.
Through the darkness, a spark flares bright,
Guiding our souls through the velvet night.

Behind the bars, where dreams entwine,
The fire beckons in its warm design.
Each flicker tells of tales we yearn,
In the glow, our hidden hearts burn.

With every flame, a promise is cast,
For the future waiting, true love steadfast.
Enchanted and bold, we'll find our way,
Through the confines, to brighter days.

Together we'll rise, spirits set free,
Enchanted flames, a fierce jubilee.
Beyond the bars, our vision gleams,
Igniting the world, fulfilling dreams.

Flickering Insights from the Moonlit Den

In the moonlit den where shadows play,
Flickering insights guide our way.
Each beam a whisper, soft yet clear,
Illuminating paths we hold dear.

Between the trees, the night unfolds,
Stories awaken, secrets retold.
In the silence, wisdom softly chimes,
Echoes of ancient, forgotten rhymes.

Flickering light dances on leaves,
Nurturing dreams that the heart believes.
In this sacred space, we explore,
What the night has to offer and more.

With every glance, the world reveals,
A tapestry woven of sacred deals.
Through moments shared, truth is drawn,
Flickering insights greet the dawn.

In shadows deep, we find our place,
Connected to nature's loving grace.
In the moonlit den, we shall remain,
Flickering insights, our sweet refrain.

Glimmers in the Sorceress's Sanctuary

In shadows deep, where whispers hum,
A sorceress waits, her secrets spun.
Glimmers flicker, soft and bright,
In her sanctuary, the heart takes flight.

Potions brew in glassy vaults,
Mystic tongues weave tales of faults.
Magic dances, a swirling dream,
In the stillness, echoes seem.

Her wand traces sigils in the air,
With every stroke, she shows her care.
The light cascades, a silver stream,
Weaving through the night's soft gleam.

All who enter feel the pull,
Of whispers soft, the air so cool.
Ancient stories call the brave,
To seek the fortunes they might save.

In every glint, a tale unfolds,
Of love and loss, of adventures bold.
Glimmers in the sanctuary's heart,
Where every spell is a work of art.

Cages of Nightfall and Flickering Flames

Nightfall descends, wrapping the land,
With cages of shadows, darkness so grand.
Flickering flames dance in the night,
Whispering secrets, igniting delight.

The moon hangs low, a watchful eye,
Over the whispers of the sky.
Fires crackle in a timeless song,
Calling the lost, where they belong.

With each flicker, a story's told,
Of hearts once brave, of spirits bold.
Caged in silence, yet longing to fly,
Through the enchanted, star-specked sky.

Shapes in the dark begin to stir,
Eyes glimmer bright, in the silent blur.
Cages of night, a transient shade,
While flickering flames weave dreams unswayed.

Embers rise, igniting hope,
Guiding the lost with their gentle scope.
In the realm where shadows play,
Flickering flames light the way.

Echoes of the Mystic Lantern

In twilight's calm, the lantern glows,
Casting shadows, where magic flows.
Echoes of whispers fill the air,
Mystic wonders hidden with care.

Under the stars, secrets unfold,
Stories of the brave and the bold.
Each flicker speaks of paths untrod,
Illuminating dreams of the odd.

The night air shimmers with deep desire,
As souls gather 'round the flickering fire.
Lanterns beckon with warm embrace,
Guiding wanderers to find their place.

In shadows deep, the heart can soar,
Echoes of magic call for more.
A journey begun, with faith and light,
Through the mystic passages of the night.

With every glow, a promise stands,
In the embrace of the lantern's hands.
Echoes linger, a soft refrain,
Leading us home through joy and pain.

The Arcane Light Nestled in Shadows

Nestled in shadows, the arcane light,
Glimmers softly, banishing night.
Whispers of magic swirl through the air,
A tapestry woven with utmost care.

In corners dark, secrets reside,
Where knowledge and power both abide.
The light flickers, a subtle tease,
Inviting the seeker to uncover with ease.

Figures dance within the gloom,
Crafting spells that bid fear to bloom.
Symbols etched in the ancient stone,
Reveal the wisdom of ages unknown.

Each spark a thread in the cosmic loom,
A path through the dusk, a way to consume.
The arcane whispers guide the bold,
In shadows deep, new truths unfold.

A sanctuary of dreams so bright,
Nestled within the fabric of night.
Beyond the dark, where wonders gleam,
The arcane light ignites every dream.

Sinister Shadows and Glowing Reflections

In the corner lurk shadows deep,
Eyes watch closely, secrets they keep.
Whispers of darkness, soft and low,
Dare you to venture where few would go.

Reflections flicker in candle's light,
Figures dance in the dead of night.
Grasping at phantoms, fleeting yet real,
Shadows and glows share truths they conceal.

Colors bleed softly, merging the two,
Darkness and brilliance, a haunting view.
Caught in the tension of fear and delight,
Sinister shadows blend with the light.

A tapestry woven of night and day,
In every corner, a price to pay.
To understand all, you must transcend,
Hold tight the shadows; they do not end.

Caged Illuminations of the Arcane

Within the cage of whispers confined,
Illuminations of secrets entwined.
Magic flows softly, a flickering thread,
In the silence, the echoes spread.

Arcane symbols dance on the wall,
Shadows alive, they beckon and call.
Mysteries linger, dreams tethered tight,
A prisoner's hope in the still of night.

Light through the bars casts a haunting lore,
Each glimmer reveals what came before.
Hidden in depths, the truth starts to gleam,
Caged illuminations weave a dark dream.

What lies beyond is a question unasked,
Each spell and enchantment is carefully masked.
In the heart of the cage, the shadows weave lore,
Illuminations spark, forever to soar.

The Bewitched Glow Behind Gossamer Veils

Behind silky veils that shimmer and sway,
Lies a bewitched glow that calls you to stay.
Woven with magic, secrets concealed,
In the soft light, all dark truths revealed.

Gossamer threads hold stories untold,
With every flutter, a legend unfolds.
A flicker of warmth in the mist of the night,
Guides you to wonders hidden from sight.

The air thick with whispers, a gentle embrace,
Inviting the wanderer into this place.
Where shadows entwine with luminescent sighs,
Bewitched by the glow, where the heart never lies.

Embrace the allure, let it capture your soul,
Through the veils of enchantment, surrender control.
For in such moments, the world fades away,
And all that remains is the magic at play.

Enigmas Held Within the Candlelit Grate

In the grate where flickering flames weave,
Enigmas arise, too subtle to believe.
Whispers of stories hidden from view,
Within the flames, old histories brew.

Each spark a question, a puzzle to find,
Where shadows breathe softly, secrets unwind.
Candlelit warmth wraps around the night,
Casting a glow on the path to the light.

The ember's secrets, etched in their glow,
Held within silence, the tales overflow.
Time stands still as the flickers ignite,
Enigmas whispering in the heart of the night.

In the dance of the flames, mysteries play,
Illusions of truth both fragile and fey.
To peer in the depths is to challenge fate,
As enigmas held stir within the grate.

www.ingramcontent.com/pod-product-compliance
Ingram Content Group UK Ltd.
Pitfield, Milton Keynes, MK11 3LW, UK
UKHW021650200125
4194UKWH00003B/51